WELCOME TO MY COUNTRY

Welcome to BOLIVIA

Gareth Stevens Publishing
A WORLD ALMANAC EDUCATION GROUP COMPANY

Written by
NG LI-SAN

Edited by
MELVIN NEO

Edited in USA by
JENETTE DONOVAN GUNTLY

Designed by
GEOSLYN LIM

Picture research by
SUSAN JANE MANUEL
THOMAS KHOO

First published in North America in 2005 by
Gareth Stevens Publishing
A World Almanac Education Group Company
330 West Olive Street, Suite 100
Milwaukee, Wisconsin 53212 USA

Please visit our web site at
www.garethstevens.com
For a free color catalog describing
Gareth Stevens Publishing's list of high-quality
books and multimedia programs,
call 1-800-542-2595 (USA) or
1-800-387-3178 (Canada).
Gareth Stevens Publishing's fax: (414) 332-3567.

© **MARSHALL CAVENDISH INTERNATIONAL (ASIA)**
PRIVATE LIMITED 2005
Originated and designed by
Times Editions Marshall Cavendish
An imprint of Marshall Cavendish International (Asia) Pte Ltd
A member of Times Publishing Limited
Times Centre, 1 New Industrial Road
Singapore 536196
http://www.marshallcavendish.com/genref

Library of Congress Cataloging-in-Publication Data
Ng, Li-San.
Welcome to Bolivia / by Ng Li-San.
p. cm. — (Welcome to my country)
Includes bibliographical references and index.
ISBN 0-8368-3126-8 (lib. bdg.)
1. Bolivia — Juvenile literature. I. Title. II. Series.
F3308.5.N55   2005
984—dc22   2004056489

Printed in Singapore

1 2 3 4 5 6 7 8 9 09 08 07 06 05

PICTURE CREDITS
Agence French Presse: 15 (middle & bottom)
ANA Photo & Press Agency: 7, 20, 34, 40
Art Directors & TRIP Photo Library: 4, 17,
  22, 25, 36, 41
Bolivian Photo Agency: 44 (both)
Focus Team Italy: 1, 5, 18, 27 (top), 39, 43
Getty Images/Hulton Archive: 13, 14
Eduardo Gil: 27 (bottom), 32
The Hutchison Picture Library: 10, 30 (bottom)
Sylvia Cordaiy Photo Library Ltd: cover,
  3 (top), 8, 26, 45
Topham Picturepoint: 12, 16, 37
Mireille Vautier: 2, 3 (middle), 6, 15 (top), 19,
  21, 23, 24, 28, 29, 30 (top), 31, 33, 35, 38
Alison Wright: 3 (bottom), 9, 11

Digital Scanning by Superskill Graphics Pte Ltd

Contents

Words that appear in the glossary are printed in **boldface** type the first time they occur in the text.

Welcome to Bolivia!

The **Republic** of Bolivia is named after Simón Bolívar, a South American hero. In the past, the Tiwanaku **Empire** built beautiful temples near Lake Titicaca. The Incas and Spanish also built many beautiful buildings in the region. Let's learn about Bolivia and its people!

Opposite: Fresh fruits and vegetables are sold at outdoor markets similar to this one in Potosí.

Below: Children stand outside their school in Yacuces, Santa Cruz. Many poor children in the countryside do not go to school.

The Flag of Bolivia

The flag of Bolivia has been used since 1851. The flag's red band stands for war heroes. The yellow band is for Bolivia's rich minerals, and the green band is for Bolivia's many plants. In the center is Bolivia's national symbol.

5

The Land

Bolivia has an area of 424,164 square miles (1,098,581 square kilometers). Its neighbors are the countries of Brazil, Paraguay, Argentina, Chile, and Peru. Bolivia's Andes Mountains are divided into two main *cordilleras* (kohr-dee-YEH-rahs), or mountain chains. The chains are the Cordillera Oriental and the Cordillera Occidental. Bolivia's highest peak is Mount Sajama. It stands 21,463 feet (6,542 meters) high.

Below: Few plants grow during the dry season in Bolivia's Andes Mountains.

The Altiplano is a highland region in the west. It contains the Uyuni Salt Flat, a huge salt desert. The Yungas, a region of thick rain forests, is found east of the cordilleras. The Oriente region is in the east of Bolivia. It has **savannas**, plains, forests, swamps, and jungles. Bolivia has several large rivers, including the Beni, Mamoré, and Iténez Rivers. Lake Titicaca , in the west of Bolivia, is the world's highest **navigable** lake. Other important lakes in the country include Lake Rogagua and Lake Rogoaguado.

Above: Crystal clear waters greet visitors to Lake Chalviri in Oruro, which is high up in the Bolivian Andes Mountains.

Climate

Different areas of Bolivia have different climates. In the Andes Mountains, the average temperature is between 45° and 52° Fahrenheit (7° and 11° Celsius). At night, it is colder. Near Lake Titicaca, daytime temperatures can rise to 70° F (21° C). On the Altiplano, cold winds blow all year. The Oriente region is hot. Temperatures can reach 80° F (27° C). The Yungas are cool and damp.

Below: Rabbit-like animals called viscachas live on Fisherman's Island, which is in the middle of the Uyuni Salt Flat in Potosí.

Plants and Animals

Many plants grow in Bolivia, except in the salty southern parts of the Altiplano. In the northern Altiplano, plants such as cactus shrubs grow. **Native** khena and quishuara trees grow in other areas of Bolivia. Trees such as cedar, laurel, and green pine and some plants used for medicines grow in the Yungas valleys.

Bolivia has many animals, including alpacas, monkeys, jaguars, armadillos, and capybaras, which are the world's largest rodents. Birds such as Andean condors live in the country as well.

History

Human bones between 10,000 and 12,000 years old have been found in the Andes, but it is believed people settled there much earlier.

From between A.D. 200 and 600, the Tiwanaku Empire settled the land near Lake Titicaca. They were very clever and used new methods to grow crops. They also built the Akapana Pyramid and other large stone buildings.

Below: This golden mask dates from before the 900s A.D. It shows a god that was worshiped by both the Tiwanaku and Inca people.

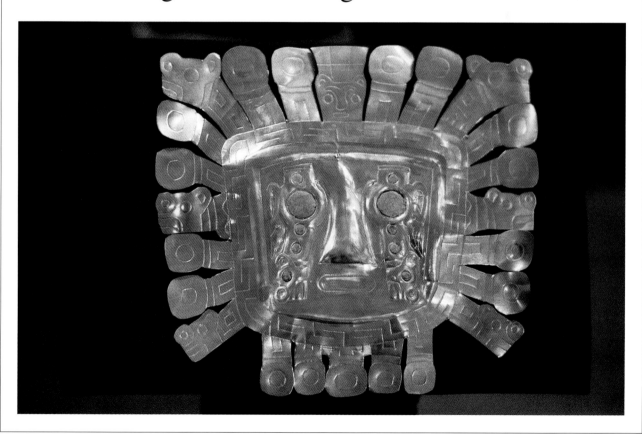

Inca and Spanish Rule

By A.D. 1200, the Tiwanaku Empire had broken up. Smaller kingdoms took its place. They were later taken over by the Quechua-speaking Incas from Peru. The Spanish took control in the 1500s. They made native Aymara people and Quechua people work in silver mines, where many of them died. In the early 1800s, people in cities such as La Paz and Sucre began to fight the Spanish. Bolivia finally won its **independence** on August 6, 1825.

Above:
This stone carving in the city of La Paz shows Spanish soldiers arriving in South America. In the 1800s, many South Americans fought to be free of Spanish control, including famous hero Simón Bolívar.

The Republic's Early Years

By 1846, many of the country's silver mines closed and Bolivia's economy was in poor shape. The country was rich in resources, such as **nitrates**, but the Bolivians could not mine them. In the 1840s, companies from Chile began to mine nitrates in Bolivia. Bolivia then raised **export taxes** on the nitrates. In turn, Chile took over Bolivia's port of Antofagasta. The fight over taxes led to the War of the Pacific (1879–1883). In 1884, Bolivia signed a truce with Chile.

Left: Fishermen collect the day's catch at the port of Antofagasta. In addition to the port, Bolivia also lost all of its land along the Pacific Ocean to Chile after the War of the Pacific.

Left: In July 1938, Bolivian officials went to Argentina to sign a peace treaty ending the Chaco War. Bolivia and Paraguay had fought the war over the Chaco Boreal region of Bolivia. After the war, some of the region was taken by Paraguay.

Bolivia in the Twentieth Century

After the War of the Pacific, Bolivia's Government made the economy stable and helped the mining industry grow. From 1932 to 1935, the country fought Paraguay in the Chaco War. Between 1936 and 1952, the country had many different Governments. In 1952, one political party, called the Movimento Nacionalista Revolucionario (MNR), took control. The MNR improved life for many Bolivians, especially Native Bolivians. A military Government took control in 1964. From 1978 to 1982, Bolivia had ten different Governments.

Democracy and a Better Economy

After many changes in Government, Bolivia became a **democracy** again in 1982. During the 1980s, the country's economy was in trouble. By 1985, some banks and industries almost had to shut down. Bolivia's farming industry also suffered because of bad weather. The new Government made changes to help solve the problems. In 1993, Gonzalo Sánchez de Lozada Bustamente was elected president. He **privatized** many companies. People from other countries then put money into the companies.

Left: General Hugo Bánzer Suárez ruled Bolivia from 1971 to 1978. His rule was harsh, and many people were killed. In 1997, Bánzer was elected president. He became ill and left office in 2001. In 2002, Gonzalo Sánchez de Lozada Bustamente was reelected president.

Antonio José de Sucre Alcalá (1795–1830)

Antonio José de Sucre Alcalá served as Simón Bolívar's general in the **rebellion** against Spain. Sucre freed Ecuador and Peru before taking over Bolivia in 1825. The next year, he became Bolivia's first president.

Antonio José de Sucre Alcalá

Víctor Paz Estenssoro (1907–2001)

Víctor Paz Estenssoro helped set up the political party MNR in 1941. He was elected president in 1952. He is known for making many social and economic changes. He was reelected president in 1960 and again in 1985.

Víctor Paz Estenssoro

Lidia Gueiler Tejada (1921–)

From 1956 to 1964, Lidia Gueiler Tejada served in **parliament**. In 1979, she became Bolivia's first female president. In 1980, a military group forced her out of office. She later served as Bolivia's **ambassador** to West Germany and then Venezuela.

Lidia Gueiler Tejada

Government and the Economy

The Government of Bolivia has three branches. The executive branch makes rules for the Government and also runs it. It is headed by the president, vice president, and a cabinet of ministers, or advisors. The legislative, or lawmaking, branch consists of a parliament called the National Congress. The congress has two parts, the Chamber of Senators and the Chamber of Deputies.

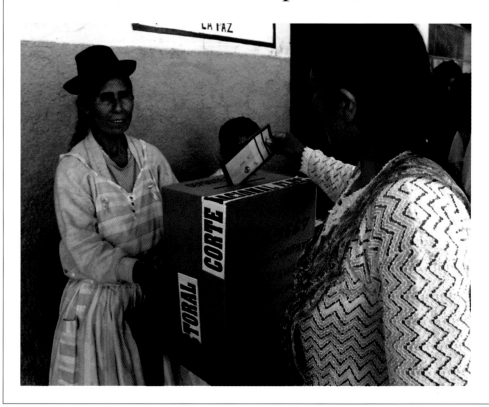

Left: This Native woman is voting for her choice of mayor in December 1999. She is in Coripata, which is a town in the La Paz region.

Bolivia's judiciary branch runs the court system. It includes a Supreme Court, a system of lower courts, and a **Constitutional** Tribunal. The tribunal is a court. One of its duties is to decide whether the laws passed in the country are legal under Bolivia's constitution.

Above: Since 1904, this building in La Paz has been used to house Bolivia's National Congress. Members of the National Congress are elected to five-year terms in office.

Local Government

The country is divided into nine regions called departments. A prefect, or chief official, runs each department, which is divided into smaller regions as well.

The Economy

Bolivia has many natural resources, such as minerals, **petroleum**, natural gas, and forests. Because of a lack of money and poor means of shipping the products, the country has not been able to use these resources. In the late 1900s, Bolivia's economy was changed. After some companies were privatized, many people put money into the companies. These and other changes helped the country's economy grow stronger.

Below: Farmers sell their vegetables and fruits at a market in Santa Cruz. Many Bolivian farmers can only grow enough food to feed themselves and their families.

Left: A worker checks a gauge at an oil **refinery** in Santa Cruz. The country's oil fields are located in Santa Cruz, Chuquisaca, and Tarija.

Farming and Mining

Part of Bolivia's economy depends on farming. In the Altiplano, crops such as potatoes, wheat, and corn are grown. In the Oriente region, soybeans are grown. In the Yungas, crops include bananas, coffee, and oranges. Some poor farmers in the Yungas grow coca plants, but the government is trying to stop them. Coca leaves are often used to make cocaine, which is an illegal drug.

Some Bolivians mine silver and tin. Gold is now an important export, too. Bolivia also has zinc, lead, and iron ore.

People and Lifestyle

More than half of Bolivians are from Native groups, such as the Aymara, Quechua, or Guaraní. In the 1500s, Spanish people arrived. Today, many Bolivians are *mestizos* (mays-TEE-sohs), or people with **ancestors** from Native and Spanish or other European groups. Some people moved to Bolivia from countries such as Japan, England, and Germany. **Mennonites** moved to Bolivia from Mexico and Paraguay.

Below: These Bolivian families are celebrating Mother's Day in a shopping mall in La Paz.

Social Classes in Bolivia

Bolivia has three social classes. The upper class is very small and is mostly made up of high-ranking government officials and successful businesspeople. Most of them have Spanish ancestors. The middle class is mostly made up of professionals, such as doctors, teachers, and shopkeepers. A few Native people and many mestizos are in the middle class. The lower class is mostly made up of Native people. Most of them work in factories, in mines, or on farms.

Family Life

In Bolivia, families are very important. Many large families, including parents, children, grandparents, aunts, uncles, and cousins, depend on each other for support. Bolivian women are the center of their families. In some households, the women earn the money. In cities, many women hold good jobs. Some women hold important government positions. Many Native women and women living in the countryside own businesses selling items such as food, crafts, and different kinds of cloth.

Left: Guests throw confetti at a newly married couple in front of a church in La Paz.

Health care

In cities, most Bolivians receive health care. In the Oriente region and other **rural** areas, there are not enough health care workers. Most people receive care only when doctors and nurses travel through the area. Because of the lack of care, many people in the Oriente suffer from serious diseases, such as malaria. International groups are working hard to improve health care in Bolivia.

Above: A group of Bolivians wait for a parade to begin. Most men and women in Bolivia live an average of sixty-five years.

Education

Bolivian children begin school at age six or seven. They must attend primary school for eight years. Many children in poor rural areas do not finish primary school. They must work to help support their families. The government started a program called "Education for All" to help almost all students finish primary school. Local and international groups are helping with funds to train teachers, build schools, and help poor children.

Below:
Two students do their homework at a park in Sucre. Most students in Bolivia finish primary school by age fourteen.

Secondary School and Universities

After primary school, many Bolivian students choose to attend secondary school. Students may choose either a **technical** program or a general studies program. Both programs last four years and are divided into two-year sections.

After completing secondary school, many students choose to attend colleges or universities. The country has many technical colleges and teacher training colleges as well as many public and private universities.

Above: After school, groups of high school girls in Sucre walk to the bus stop. White is a common color for school uniforms in Bolivia.

Religion

The official religion of Bolivia is the Roman Catholic religion. Almost all Bolivians are Catholics. Some people in the country are Protestant Christians, Jews, or Mormons. Some Bolivians believe in native religions.

The Roman Catholic Church in Bolivia has tried to help society by setting up groups to study important subjects, such as the family, youth, education, culture, and social justice.

Below: Vendors sell flowers and religious images outside the Copacabana Church near Lake Titicaca .

Native Beliefs

In Bolivia, the Catholic Church and Native religions have influenced each other. For some native Quechua people, for instance, the Christian cross is also a symbol of some mountain gods and of **fertility**. Native religions teach that spirits cause events such as diseases, earthquakes, and rain. Many people offer **sacrifices** to those spirits in an attempt to control events around them.

Above: Catholics pray in the Church of San Francisco in La Paz.

Below: Mennonites stand outside their Santa Cruz home.

Language

Bolivia has three official languages: Spanish, Aymara, and Quechua. Most Bolivians speak Spanish, which is the country's main official language. Some Bolivians, mostly Native people, speak Spanish and also speak Aymara and Quechua. In far-off regions of Bolivia, some people may not speak Spanish.

Bolivia has more than thirty different languages. Chiquitano and Guaraní are spoken in the east. Tacana, Cavineña, and Ignaciano are spoken in Beni.

Below: Many Bolivians, such as these people in Cochabamba, take time to read the newspaper every day.

Left: An Aymara woman talks on a phone at her job in Santa Cruz. Today, most Aymara and Quechua people speak their native languages and also speak Spanish.

Literature

Bolivia has a rich literary history. The country's most famous Quechua work of literature is a play called *Ollantay*. It is about the romance of an Inca princess and Ollanta, a general. In 1903, Alcides Arguedas (1879–1946) published one of Bolivia's earliest novels, *Pisagua*. Another well-known Bolivian novel is *Los deshabitados,* written by Marcelo Quiroga Santa Cruz (1931–1980).

Arts

Bolivia has a rich artistic history. The Tiwanaku people are known for the grand temples they built. Many human and animal sculptures were carved into the temples. Tiwanaku pottery is also famous. Most pieces were painted in black, red, and yellow with pictures of animals, human heads, and many shapes on them. Later, the Incas built grand buildings, such as the Palacio del Inca on an island in Lake Titicaca.

Above: A blend of Native and Spanish styles can be seen in this painting *La Virgen del Cerro*, or *Virgin of the Hill*.

Left: A Native girl wears a handmade hat that combines both Spanish and Native styles.

Left: An example of mestizo baroque style can be seen on this carving in the Church of San Lorenzo in Potosí. Many old pieces of religious art made in Bolivia were covered with gold and silver.

Spanish and Native Art

The Spanish brought European styles of art to Bolivia. Beginning in the 1500s, Native Bolivian artists began to build churches and create religious paintings and sculptures in the Spanish style. They mixed in Native styles of art, too. The new style of art was called mestizo **baroque**. Today, sculptures by Marina Núñez del Prado are famous. Alfredo La Placa, Oscar Pantoja, and Gil Imaná are other well-known Bolivian artists.

Music

The Native peoples of the Altiplano and the Andes have a long musical history. **Traditional** instruments include flutes, trumpets, and drums. New instruments were brought to Bolivia by the Spanish, including harps, violins, mandolins, and *charangos* (cha-RAHN-gohs), which are guitars made from armadillo shells. Traditional flutes such as the *siku* (SEE-koo) are often still played in folk music.

Below: At a festival in La Paz, Aymara men play the *tarka* (TAHR-kah), which is a traditional wind instrument made from wood.

Museums and Cultural Centers

Bolivia has many museums and cultural centers. In large cities, many private art galleries, theaters, and museums display cloth, metalwork, and modern jewelry, sculpture, and paintings. Museums in La Paz include the National Museum of **Archaeology**, the Kusillo Children's Museum, and the National Museum of Art. Art performances and art shows are also held at cultural centers in La Paz, such as the Bolivian American Center.

Above: Bolivians in bright costumes perform a dance during the festival of Santa Rosa in Potosí. Dances are an important part of Bolivian festivals and celebrations. Traditional Aymara dances include the *cueca* (KWAY-kah) and the *sikuri* (see-KOOH-ree).

Leisure

Bolivians spend most of their free time with friends and family. In cities, many people go to the movies. Some wealthy Bolivians in cities enjoy going to discos and Internet cafés and eating meals at restaurants. Almost all Bolivians enjoy shopping. Wealthy people near cities shop in expensive supermarkets. Most poor people shop in open-air markets.

Below: The game of *futbolín* (foot-boh-LEEN) or foosball, is popular among Bolivian boys.

Games

At outdoor restaurants in Bolivia, many people enjoy playing *sapo* (SAH-poh). In the game, players try to shoot tokens into a metal toad's mouth. In Bolivia, many women play card games, such as canasta and rummy. Some married men play card games and a dice game called *cacho* (KAH-choh). On Fridays, some of the men go to bars. Bolivian children play with marbles, dolls, slingshots, and *trompos* (TROHM-pohs), or tops.

Above: Girls play at a park in La Paz under their father's watchful eyes.

Sports

Bolivia's most popular sport is soccer. The Bolivian Football Association was founded in 1925. It governs the sport of soccer in Bolivia. The association joined the Fédération Internationale de Football Association (FIFA), which is the worldwide soccer association, in 1926. Famous Bolivian soccer teams include Real Santa Cruz and Oriente Petrolero. Bolivia's national team took part in the FIFA World Cup in 1994 and the Copa América finals in 1997.

Below: Soccer is played by Bolivians all over the country, including by these Native women in the city of Copacabana. Bolivia's women's team takes part in the Sudamericano Feminina, which is a competition for women from South America.

One famous Bolivian soccer star is Marco Etcheverry, who plays for the D.C. United, a U.S. team. The Tahuichi Academy in Bolivia has offered many talented poor children an education and soccer training, including Etcheverry.

Sports such as volleyball, basketball, automobile racing, cycling, and boxing are also popular in Bolivia. In the 2003 Pan American Games, cyclist Benjamin Martinez and two racquetball players, Paola Nuñez and Carola Loma Santos, all won bronze medals.

Holidays and Festivals

Bolivian festivals are colorful with lots of music and dancing. From February to March, many carnivals are held before **Lent**. In Oruro, many musicians and dancers take part in a parade. They often wear costumes with masks made of feathers, tin cans, cloth, and other materials. Dances performed during the parade include the *morenada* (mor-ren-NAH-dah). It tells the story of African slaves forced to work in Spanish mines.

Below: Believers stand around the statue of the Virgin of Copacabana. A festival in honor of the Virgin Mary is held each August on the shores of Lake Titicaca.

During the religious festival of Holy Week in March or April, many people walk from La Paz to Copacabana. In May or June, the festival of El Gran Poder is celebrated in La Paz in honor of Jesus Christ. Colorful parades and music and dance competitions are held. Each August in Cochabamba, the feasts of the Virgin of Copacabana and the Virgin of Urkupiña are held. On the first two days of November, Bolivians celebrate All Saints' Day by visiting loved ones' graves and leaving flowers.

Above: A man in a scary mask takes part in a parade in Copacabana. A dance called the *diablada* (dee-ah-BLAH-dah) is often performed during Oruro's carnivals. The dancers wear devil masks.

Food

Bolivian food uses the country's wide range of farm produce, including over one hundred kinds of potatoes. It also includes **quinoa** and many kinds of peppers, including *locoto* (loh-KOH-toh) and *ulupica* (ooh-loo-PEE-kah) peppers. *Quirquiña* (keer-KEEN-nya), a native herb, is also used. Many dishes mix Spanish and Native cooking styles.

Below: Bakers at street stalls sell their freshly baked breads. Different kinds of wheat are used to prepare Bolivian breads.

Chupe de papaliza (CHOO-pay day pah-pah-LEE-zah) is a Bolivian soup. It is made of broad beans, squash, and papalizas, which are yellow potatoes.

Popular Bolivian meat dishes include roast pig, chicken and pork stews, and spicy chicken dishes. *Salteñas* (sahl-TEHN-nyas) are turnovers filled with meat, olives, eggs, peppers, and spices. *Majao* (mah-JOW) is roast beef or beef jerky and rice. The dish is served with fried **plantain**, egg, and **cassava**.

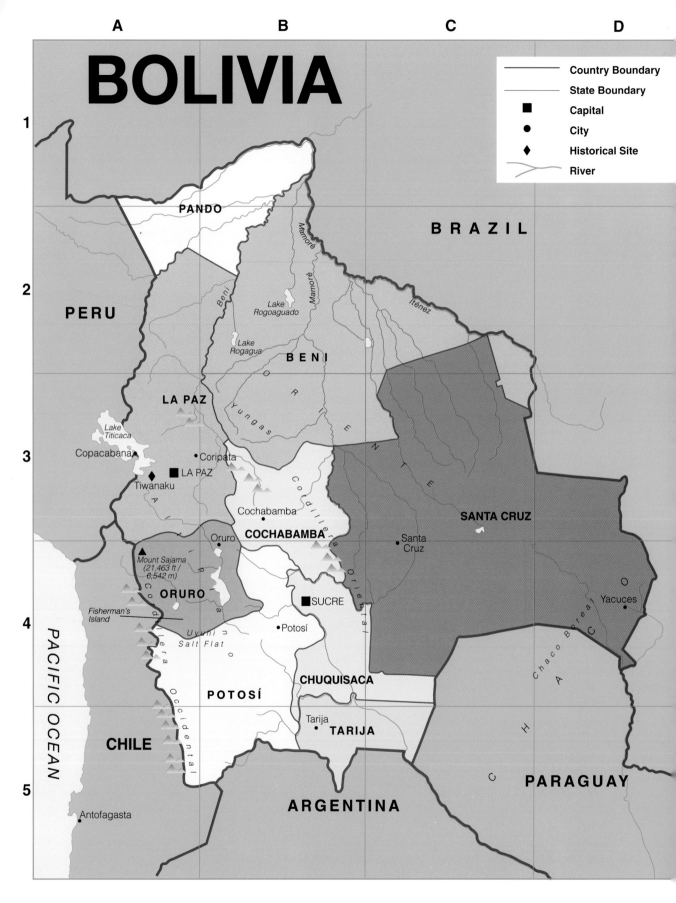

Above: Bolivians wear colorful costumes during the festival of the Virgin of Copacabana.

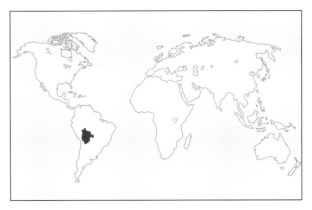

Quick Facts

Official Name	República de Bolivia (Republic of Bolivia)
Capital	Sucre (legal capital; seat of the judiciary); La Paz (administrative capital)
Official Languages	Aymara, Quechua, and Spanish
Population	8,724,156 (July 2004 estimate)
Land Area	424,164 square miles (1,098,581 square km)
Departments	Beni, Chuquisaca, Cochabamba, La Paz, Oruro, Pando, Potosí, Santa Cruz, and Tarija
Highest Point	Mount Sajama 21,463 feet (6,542 meters)
Major Rivers	Beni, Iténez, Mamoré
Famous Leaders	General Antonio Jóse de Sucre, Víctor Paz Estenssoro, General Hugo Bánzer Suárez
Major Religions	Roman Catholic, Protestant, Native religions
Holidays	Holy Week (March or April); Good Friday (April); El Gran Poder (May or June); feast of Virgin of Copacabana (August); feast of Virgin of Urkupiña (August); Independence Day (August 6); All Saints' Day (November 1 and 2); Christmas (December 25)
Currency	Boliviano (7.93 BOB = U.S. $1 in July 2004)

Opposite: This statue guards the Kalasasaya Temple, made by the Tiwanaku people.

Glossary

ambassador: official who represents his or her government in another country.

ancestors: family members from the past, farther back than grandparents.

archaeology: study of old items, such as pottery, left by people from long ago.

baroque: a style of the 1600s and 1700s that used fancy, flowery designs.

cassava: a root that is cooked and eaten.

constitutional: regarding a nation's set of laws, including citizen rights.

democracy: a government in which the citizens elect their leaders by vote.

empire: a very large collection of lands or regions ruled by one group.

export taxes: fees charged on products sold and shipped to another country.

fertility: ability to feed or produce life.

independence: being free from the control of others.

Lent: the Christian season of fasting during the forty days before Easter.

Mennonites: groups of Christians who believe in living a simple life.

native: belonging to a land or region by having first grown or been born there.

navigable: suitable for travel by boat.

nitrates: a type of mineral salt often used as a fertilizer or to preserve meat.

parliament: elected government group that makes the laws for their country.

petroleum: natural oil from the ground, before it is refined.

plantain: a fruit similar to a banana.

privatized: taken from the government and given to a private company.

quinoa: a type of grain from the Andes.

rebellion: a fight against a government or a ruler.

refinery: a factory in which unwanted things are removed, such as from oil.

republic: a country in which citizens elect their own lawmakers.

rural: relating to the countryside.

sacrifices: offerings of valuable things, often animals or people, to a god.

savannas: dry grasslands.

technical: relating to using machines or science to perform a job or task.

traditional: relating to customs or styles passed down through the generations.

More Books to Read

Bolivia. Discovering South America Series. LeeAnne Gelletly (Mason Crest Publishers)

Bolivia: First Reports series. Cynthia Klingel and Robert B. Noyed (Compass Point Books)

Bolivia. Fiesta! series. Grolier Educational staff (Scholastic Library)

The Emerald Lizard: Fifteen Latin American Tales to Tell in English and Spanish. Pleasant Despain (August House Publishers)

Golden Tales: Myths, Legends, and Folktales from Latin America. Lulu Delacre (Scholastic Books)

The Incas. History Opens Windows series. Jane Shuter (Heinemann)

Messengers of Rain and Other Poems of Latin America. Claudia M. Lee, editor (Groundwood Books)

Llamas. Early Bird Nature series. Dorothy Hinshaw Patent (Lerner)

South America. Continents series. Myra Weatherly (Child's World Inc)

The Spanish Exploration of South America. Exploration and Discovery series. Mark McKain (Mason Crest Publishers)

Videos

Full Circle with Michael Palin: Chile/ Bolivia and Peru. (PBS Home Video)

Globe Trekker: Bolivia. (555 Productions)

NOVA: Secrets of Lost Empires – Inca (WGBH Boston Video)

Simon Bolivar (Schlessinger Media)

Web Sites

news.bbc.co.uk/1/hi/world/americas/ country_profiles/1210487.stm

www.crystalinks.com/laketiticaca.html

www.sciencedaily.com/encyclopedia/ bolivia

www.waterhistory.org/histories/tiwanaku/

Due to the dynamic nature of the Internet, some web sites stay current longer than others. To find additional web sites, use a reliable search engine with one or more of the following keywords to help you locate information about Bolivia. Keywords: *Aymara, Inca, La Paz, Lake Titicaca, Simon Bolivar, and Tiwanaku.*

Index